# LIZ JOHNSON ARTUR

The Tate Photography Series is a celebration of international and British photography in the Tate collection and an introduction to some of the most significant photographers at work today.

Each book focuses on an individual photographer and features a specially selected sequence of photographs, an introduction by a Tate curator, and a conversation with the photographer. These collaborations between living artists and experts enrich our understanding of photography and its connection to everyday life, and move from city streets to seashores, across landscapes and subcultures, through identities and interiors, in a visual travelogue of our world today.

Set against the various social, political and cultural issues of our time, the theme for Series One is Community and Solidarity, which brings together four photographers, unrelated as individual artists yet unified here by their work. A Ghanaian-Russian photographer joins Black Lives Matter street protests in London, an artist-activist in New Delhi chronicles women's emancipatory struggles, a South-African's camera locates queer lives in rural townships, while a Finnish-British photographer captures the community spirit in the North-East of England as perhaps only an émigré can.

Work from several continents is brought together, connected by shared practice. In all of these locations and environments, each imbued with unique struggles and dangers, a commonality of human character and strength inspired by community and solidarity is portrayed, permitting glimpses of joy and hope.

Series One

1:1     **LIZ JOHNSON ARTUR**
1:2     **SIRKKA-LIISA KONTTINEN**
1:3     **SABELO MLANGENI**
1:4     **SHEBA CHHACHHI**

# LIZ JOHNSON ARTUR

Edited by
Yasufumi Nakamori

First published 2022 by order of the Tate Trustees
by Tate Publishing, a division of Tate Enterprises Ltd,
Millbank, London SW1P 4RG
www.tate.org.uk/publishing

© Tate Enterprises Ltd 2022
Artworks by Liz Johnson Artur © the artist 2022

A catalogue record for this book is available from
the British Library
ISBN 978 1 84976 801 6

Distributed in the United States and Canada
by ABRAMS, New York

Library of Congress Control Number applied for

Series Editors: Simon Armstrong and Yasufumi
Nakamori
Senior Editor: Nicola Bion
Production: Bill Jones
Picture Research: Emma O'Neill
Designed by Sarah Boris
Colour reproduction by Westerham Press, London
Printed and bound in the UK by Westerham Press,
London

Cover: *Time don't run here* 2020

# CONTENTS

6    INTRODUCTION

8    IN CONVERSATION

14   PLATES

64   CREDITS

64   ACKNOWLEDGEMENTS

# INTRODUCTION

In spring 2020, Liz Johnson Artur photographed countless protestors at Black Lives Matter (BLM) protests in London. The black and white and colour prints included in this publication are among the numerous prints (twenty-six of which are in the Tate collection) that comprise *Time don't run here* (2020). The work forms part of what Johnson Artur calls her *Black Balloon Archive*, the vast body of ongoing work she, as a Ghanaian-Russian diaspora photographer based in the UK, has made since the 1990s depicting people in Africa, and of the African and Caribbean diaspora, mostly in South East London, New York, Paris and further afield.

After joining the protests that began on 30 May 2020 in her neighbourhood of Peckham Rye, South East London, Johnson Artur was motivated to show her solidarity with, and photograph, BLM protestors in Vauxhall, Westminster and Trafalgar Square. She decided to print the work on the A4-sized leaves from the 1968 braille edition of Iris Murdoch's *The Red and The Green* (1965) and the A3-sized leaves of the 1975 braille edition of John Harris's *Ride out the Storm: A Novel of Dunkirk* (1975), both braille books she had previously collected. The former is a historical novel, set at the time of the Easter Rising of 1916, about an Anglo-Irish family and their differing religious affiliations and views on the relations between England and Ireland. Harris's book describes the massive evacuation of more than a quarter of a million Allied soldiers across the English Channel into the UK from the Battle of Dunkirk against the Nazis around the French port of Dunkirk in 1940. For Johnson Artur it is significant that in its materiality and content *Time don't run here* contains multiple transhistorical references to difference, conflict and resistance, both historic and contemporary. Looking closely at the prints from the series, one can see the braille marks beneath the photographic images. Thus, *Time don't run here* embodies the photographer's unique and ongoing pursuits in experimenting with photographic materials, processes and presentations (unique photobooks and photozines are the formats Johnson Artur has championed frequently). This significant work is among the most recent and best examples of the documentary aspect of her wide-ranging photographic practice, which includes abstract darkroom experimentations.

In her non-commercial artistic work, Johnson Artur rarely photographs people close to her: the vast majority of her subjects are strangers. Sometimes she approaches them, explaining who she is and that the images will become part of her artwork or archive. Other times she feels that consent is implied because the participant is aware that they are being photographed; she also notes that at the Black Lives Matter protests, 'people were there to be seen'.[1] She pictures protestors in their best light and in a dignified fashion.

For Johnson Artur, it is important that Black Lives Matter protests are recorded and that these records are visible to the public for many generations. She stresses the importance of seeing positive images of oneself and one's community reflected back in visual culture: 'there is a generation of kids who don't have time to wait'. For her, *Time don't run here* is a work about London as much as it is about the people she depicts. The work's title and making evince her desire to show the transhistorical power of dissenting voices and protests through experiments with photography.

*Yasufumi Nakamori*
*Senior Curator, International Art (Photography), Tate*

*Emma Lewis*
*Assistant Curator, International Art, Tate*

1    All quotes from Liz Johnson Artur are taken from conversations with Tate curators Yasufumi Nakamori and Emma Lewis, 13 July 2020 and 23 September 2020.

## LIZ JOHNSON ARTUR
## AND YASUFUMI NAKAMORI
## IN CONVERSATION

YN    You were born in Bulgaria and grew up in Germany. Your father was Ghanaian. Your mother was Russian. How did your international environment help shape your vision as a photographer?

LJA    I think that my personal story reflects a lot about diaspora experience – having roots and connections to different places, keeping memories (photographs) of places and people you might not have seen or lived in. A lot of my famiy was preserved in photographs, they formed an essential part of how I heard stories being told. This experience didn't make me want to be a photographer ... I wanted to become a photographer when I discovered how I could take and make my own photographs, being able to not just 'witness the moment', but also to go through a process of processing, printing the photograph. The physical engagement with my photographs and my experience of photographs being an essential tool to bring out stories – this is what informs most of my work.

YN    The year 2020 saw the emergence of the Black Lives Matter movement and the Covid-19 pandemic. What was the year like for you?

LJA    The beginning of 2020 still had the energy of 2019. I had a show in St Louis that opened up in February, *Liz Johnson Artur: Dusha*, which had travelled from the Brooklyn Museum. All seemed good. Then, when I got back to London, we had our first lockdown. I had access to a darkroom and some black and white film, and a lot of the mood – the strangeness of that time, the absence of people on the street – I took in by taking pictures and spending time in the darkroom. For me it was actually a very fruitful time! My pictures are very much about what I see, but what this time really brought out was a need to show in my work how I 'feel' about it. 2020 helped me to push this need in my work.

YN    What did the 'suspended' time of the two national lockdowns in the UK bring to you?

**LJA**   I wasn't at the receiving end of things when they starting to fall apart. I had my family, my work, a home and most importantly, time. I was one of the lucky ones.

**YN**   How did you come to create your work *Time don't run here*? And what does the title mean in the context of the year 2020?

**LJA**   I was pretty locked down for almost three months in Brighton, seeing only my family. But when I heard about the first BLM march, I had to go to London. My daughter went with me – the majority of demonstrators were young people.

When I was taking pictures I tried to look at faces, signs, places – not wanting to miss anything – and to preserve these moments, I decided to connect them with 'time'. I can't say what went through my head, but I knew that whatever pictures I took, I wanted to preserve them for the 'test of time'. The reason we still talk about the 1968 generation and demonstrations is because they were recorded for time to come, and I wanted the same connection. The title of my work comes from trying to find a way of saying '*Time don't run here* – it's up to you where you take it.' I chose Iris Murdoch's novel (in braille), because it represents time in a physical sense, having been printed in 1968, and because the words (which you can only read by touching the paper) deal with 'British History'.

**YN**   Your 2019 show in Brooklyn traced your thirty years of photo-making to your first visit to Brooklyn in 1986. The Brooklyn exhibition, even though it was compact, showed photography not only as an image and your material, but also the range of your display strategies, including photobooks, single prints and films. What about your exhibition at the South London Gallery (SLG) in 2019, *Liz Johnson Artur: If you know the beginning, the end is no trouble*? That seemed to push your Brooklyn exhibition further by showing your photographs in an architectural installation.

**LJA**   The SLG was a space I had known for a very long time, and when the possibility was there, I was like: 'If I can get the whole space, then I'm gonna use it.'

**YN**   That exhibition showed pictures from your *Black Balloon Archive*. Can you speak about that series?

LJA    The *Black Balloon Archive* is a collection of the photographs that I have made over the last thirty-five years, chronicling the everyday lives and beauty of African and African-diaspora people across London, Paris and New York, as well as countries in Africa, Europe, and the Caribbean. The *Time don't run here* photos are part of the archive.

YN    Do you see yourself in the narratives, in the pictures that you create?

LJA    I do. In terms of the photographs, I don't take narrative photographs. I don't try to. But the way I approached SLG was to think of it as a narrative that begins somewhere. The photographs are almost like my elements – I create them, I have them, I sometimes go back and pull some out. Or sometimes I'll go out and take some pictures. And in terms of telling the narrative, I start sometimes rephotographing things, simply because I find them interesting in the context of my work.

For me, telling the story is really about getting people into a space where they can read by themselves and also communicate and take things up. Because that's the beauty of photography. It doesn't pin you down, it allows space for your own reflections.

YN    Each of your photographs is like a fragment of the space you share, or a fragment of time you share with others. Your photography seems to speak critically when you have a group of images and there is a relation you create between you and a person photographed, and also among the pictures you take.

LJA    Yeah, and I think you see why I like to call it a kind of narrative approach – you could assemble individuals, and each individual is important for the narrative of this story. You could almost pull them from different places, different times. And in a certain way it comes out of this thing of me making my books, and actually making sense of why a picture that I took in New York makes sense next to a picture that I took in Bamako. You can say I'm the narrator of both images.

YN    Right – you are linking them up.

LJA    I like to link them up because a lot of my work has to do with encountering people. But I think by putting them together and leaving them out, whatever you take out of it is again your own narrative. At the SLG I had two books where people could write things. And what I didn't expect was for people to say they saw their aunt here, their uncle. That made me think, 'These pieces are someone's memories, and they are much closer to those memories than I am.'

YN  Let's talk about the importance of photobooks and photozines in your practice. You have made unique photobooks and photozines, and you've mentioned before that it's another format to show your work. In such a publication, each picture means something for people who go through this time-based spatial experience of flipping its pages.

LJA  A photobook or photozine is always part of how I'm trying to engage – this thing of seeing it as a whole without having this sort of direction. You know, like a photograph hasn't got a title, and one reason I didn't want a title was because I didn't want any direction. You can look at a photobook picture-by-picture or you can go back and forth, and I think that's closest to how I keep my work. I don't write down what day I took a particular photograph, or what year. And it's interesting because, since I started showing work, I've found that's one of the things people need to know or want to know. The thing is, I remember each picture in terms of the moment, how I got there, so for me the memory is, I know the year and I know which place, I just don't know the names. That would have been a whole different journey to get every name. But in order to connect with someone, you don't need to know their name. You can sometimes really just spend two seconds exchanging something, so you both go away with something richer than before. People can sense very quickly why you take a picture. So for me it's never been a thing of wanting to get a picture because I can get away with it. Instead, sometimes it's very direct, and most of the time what I try to show is interest.

YN  How do you show interest?

LJA  Now, after doing it for thirty years, I can tell you it's just by going up and saying, 'I want your picture.' But that's not a journey that I've started – it's a process and that's why my work exists on these levels, through engaging. Engaging by taking photographs, by being in situations where I have to have the courage to go up to someone and ask. It's a very humbling experience to go up to a stranger, but by now I've learned that honesty is the best way, so first of all I tell them why I'm interested. You know, a lot of the time it comes through not so much their style but how people carry themselves and in a certain way I try to tell them. If it's, let's say, what they wear, then I will comment and say: 'Your way of presenting is something that I would love to take a picture of.' And people can say yes or no. And sometimes they say yes, and I always think, 'Wow!' Really, to this day I'm amazed when people say yes.

Not all of my pictures happen like this, but the situation is one way: I see someone and I have to have my camera. These things are not always given – sometimes I see people, but I have no camera.

YN    What kind of camera do you use?

LJA    It's a Rolleiflex [medium format twin lens reflex]. I like working with this camera because it does give you some time for the subject to look at you and time for me too. You know, because I don't really look for pictures. I have pictures that I kind of sense people might not like me to take. So I do make those decisions of, 'Well, can I still use the picture?' I try not to go into situations where I take pictures of people where they don't want me to. I like to take my time and, with the Rolleiflex, you look down into the viewfinder, you have to focus.

YN    So in that sense you are shooting upside-down. And you're kind of slow, you're taking your time.

LJA    Yes, yes. I like to use frames, and what is beautiful about this camera is that I can take my time to frame my shot. I don't want people to feel that I'm just taking their picture. I'd rather slow down and give them a chance to turn around.

YN    Do you know what a picture you photograph is going to become?

LJA    I'm not quite sure when I take it whether it's going to be an installation or an object. But what I want is the idea of me going and just taking things, then putting them into a new space, and then maybe making something that I could actually take and bring to a fitting place. This process is something that I initiate with photographs. So I take pictures. And I like to start very simple, but in the end I want to have these pieces so that I can create something that has its own narrative. It's a journey that usually gets me somewhere.

YN    So are your unique photobooks and photozines, for example, also a method to show a journey?

LJA    I think so. This is how I got into photography, because I realised that there was a process that wasn't just 'Click, and there's a picture.' No, there's a whole process. I don't like to start with an idea and then just mechanically get to the end. I prefer to discover something and then go as far as I can go. And photography is very much the foundational base. What I did in the SLG was something that evolved over three days, and it evolved through me filling the whole space – there were many more pictures in the room than people actually saw. But out of this organically it came together, and that's usually what I like to have in order to start creating a book or creating maybe just a wall or an installation.

YN    Lastly, the theme that connects this issue with the other three *Tate Photography* publications is 'community and solidarity'. What does that term mean to you? And what or who is your community?

LJA    When I take pictures, I experience a lot of 'community and solidarity'. That's an everyday thing for me, because I always look out for it.

YN    And your journey does not end when you finish an installation or a book or photozine. Rather, there's a continuous dialogue between you and the people you photograph or the people who see your work, the people in your communities. This is very much evident in the format of your 2019 SLG exhibition, which is open-ended. In a way, those images are entering the minds of the visitors of your exhibit, and the images will have another life.

LJA    I had to create these dialogues in order to be able to do what I do. You know, I am for boxes and negatives, but I also want to see all those pictures – to not feel that I just take it compulsively. So for me being able to show means I can have different conversations, and one leads to another.

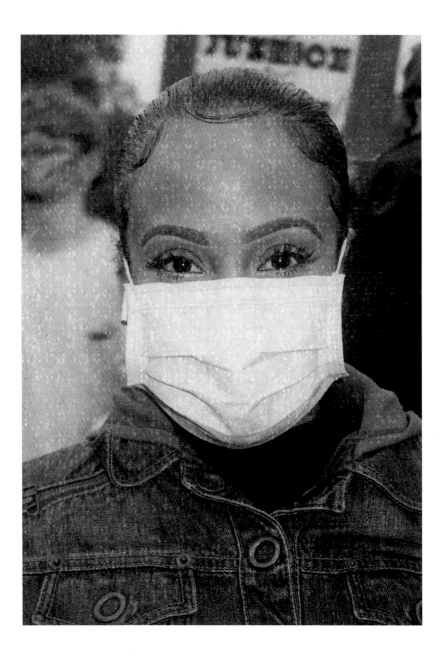

**CREDITS**

All artworks © Liz Johnson Artur 2022

*Time Don't Run Here* 2020
Photographs, inkjet prints on paper
Overall display dimensions variable

pp.15, 16–17, 21, 22, 23, 26, 38, 43, 45, 55, 59, back cover
Private collection of the artist
© Liz Johnson Artur, images courtesy the artist

pp.19, 24–5, 27, 29, 30, 31, 32, 33, 34–5, 36, 37, 39,
40, 41, 46–7, 48, 49, 50, 51, 52, 53, 56–7, 58, 60–1, 63,
front cover
Tate. Purchased with funds provided by the
Photography Acquisitions Committee 2021
© Liz Johnson Artur, images © Tate 2022

**ARTIST'S
ACKNOWLEDGEMENTS**

To all the people who came out to be seen and heard.

**EDITOR'S
ACKNOWLEDGEMENTS**

With thanks to Emma Jones and Emma Lewis
for their help in researching and preparing
this volume.

An earlier version of part of the conversation
was published in *Camera Austria*, no.149 (2020):
Liz Johnson Artur and Yasufumi Nakamori, 'A
conversation from South London', pp.51–60